B.B.C. - A National Menace

by

A.K. Chesterton

The A.K. Chesterton Trust

2013

Printed & Published in 2013.

This edition is *The A.K. Chesterton Trust Reprint Series* No. 8

ISBN: 978-0-9575403-1-6

© **The A.K. Chesterton Trust, BM Candour, London, WC1N 3XX, United Kingdom.**

Website: www.candour.org.uk

We dedicate this booklet to the founder of our movement.

A.K. Chesterton, 1899-1973

Foreword

This work by our great founder, A.K. Chesterton, was first published within *Candour* in May 1972, and appeared in booklet form the following month. It contains one of the most striking descriptions of the B.B.C. ever committed to print:

"The B.B.C. defames our past, poisons our present and places our future at desperate hazard. No nation can survive which is conditioned by a vast fifth-column serving forces which have a vested interest in its obliteration as a sovereign, independent Realm."

Four decades on, the B.B.C. has consolidated its position over public opinion. It has become one of the greatest enemies the British people have.

Until our folk realise this, there is little prospect of national rebirth. *Candour* will continue to sound the alarm until our message is clearly understood.

Colin Todd

The A.K. Chesterton Trust
April 2013

B.B.C. - A National Menace

During the fifty years of its existence the B.B.C., founded in 1922 as the British Broadcasting Company, by Godfrey Isaacs, of Marconi ill-fame, has subordinated the national interest to left-wing and largely esoteric internationalist policies and only now has any substantial number of the public begun to question its motivation. There are several reasons which account for this long record of successful indoctrination. One is that most people, being trustful, require to be jolted into an acute awareness of reality before examining the *bona fides* of an institution which in so many ways has served them well and given them much delight.

In relaying symphony concerts, in sports coverage, in non-contentious documentaries, in plays produced for their own sake and not for any ulterior purpose, above all, perhaps, in such superb series as *The Forsyte Saga*, the B.B.C. has acquired an "image" which commands respect and bestows prestige of the highest order. We should remember, however, that the men and women who supply this excellence are artists with no interest other than to give of their best.

Only when commentators selected to put over tendentious political views take the air does the atmosphere change. Civilized values then vanish, only too often, to make way for those of uncouth hirelings whose technique is sickeningly familiar. Their quarries when alive are obsequiously approached on the false pretext that the B.B.C. wishes to broadcast their opinions, whereas the real object may be to lampoon and deride them in recordings carefully edited out of sight and sound before transmission. Where the interview is "live", denigration is done through loaded questions sometimes staggering in their impertinence. Posthumous victims are even more freely savaged (as last year's ghoulish attack on Cecil Rhodes showed) without the least regard to truth or decency.

* * * *

Such tactics are not fortuitous, but part of a long propaganda campaign to slur the greatness of Britain's world achievement, denigrate her heroes, undermine the sense of nationhood of her people and reduce her to a state of vassalage in which the false values of cosmopolis are embraced. Down through the years our abandonment of power overseas, and the rapid advance of the forces of decay at home, have coincided and interacted with the ever more blatant efforts of the B.B.C., which has worked unremittingly to condition the public mind for the acceptance of our obliteration as an historical entity, entitled to the enjoyment of our thousand-year national heritage.

Those of us who watch the evil purposes being served, and do our best to make them known, have realized with something akin to despair the overwhelming odds against us in our fight against a corporation which lacks all scruples and has continuous access to many millions of minds. Our only hope, it became clear, was that the B.B.C., growing ever more confident as a result of fifty years of unbroken success, would sooner or later overplay its hand —and that is precisely what has happened. We now have to gather up all our strength to make the best possible use of the situation thereby created, which we do in the certain knowledge that unless the general attitude prevailing at Broadcasting House be radically changed, and its subversive elements eliminated, there can be no honourable, worthwhile future for Great Britain and her people.

* * * *

The first sign that the B.B.C. had begun to misjudge the extent of the nation's tolerance was observed last year. After a continuous record of helping to ditch loyalists overseas and thus facilitate Britain's abandonment of her responsibilities, Broadcasting House assumed as a matter of course that the same technique could safely he employed in the coverage of events in Northern Ireland. This turned out to be a serious miscalculation. Day after day, week after week, television viewers witnessed scenes of riot and it was extraordinary how often "shots" were shown of British soldiers (whose courage and discipline are the finest in the world) either charging juvenile mobs of stone-throwers, or cowering behind cover against attack, or else in full retreat. At the same time, while I.R.A. terrorist gangs were placing bombs in public places such as streets, restaurants and department stores, B.B.C. reporters interviewed their leaders, treating them with deference and allowing them full facilities on the air to blackguard British troops and Irish loyalists.

This was too much. There were indignant protests from every part of the United Kingdom about slanted reporting, which the B.B.C.'s Director-General, Mr. Charles Curran (successor to the egregious Hugh Greene, of whom more anon) was swift to deny. When he found this stance impossible to maintain, however, Curran issued a directive that there was to be no further I.R.A. interviews without his express consent. Why should he have done that if the criticism he had rejected lacked substance?

Meanwhile, Stormont, having taken note of those B.B.C. reporters who had recourse to dubious sources of information, informed the Director-General that they were not welcome in Northern Ireland. It was with obvious reluctance that Curran finally banned their employment in that area — a step which led to a near-revolt in

Broadcasting House. Some of the rebels were sacked: other sympathisers had too much concern for their jobs to come out openly in support. They remain!

To understand these issues it is necessary to know that the B.B.C. rebels and some of the departmental heads who tried to protect them have no interest what- ever in Catholicism or even in Irish Republicanism. They are intent upon furthering the cause of the militant New Left, which seeks the overthrow of society through violence—an objective shared by that part of the I.R.A. hard-core which is totally irreligious and uses republicanism only as a cover for the creation of social chaos.

The B.B.C. would have ridden the storm created by its handling of events in Northern Ireland had it learnt the lesson that there is a limit, as all history has shown, to the patience of the long-suffering British people. Instead, taking this acquiescence for granted, it went ahead with plans which were to offer them the biggest affront in all its annals. This was the infamous series on the British Empire.

There are three main ways in which so large a project can be approached. One is to record the towering achievements of the men and women who built and maintained the Empire with single-minded devotion to its welfare. The second is to weigh those achievements , with whatever was less well contrived—justice against injustice, service against disservice, benefits "to" as against "from", in short the total of right against the total of wrong—and so strike a balance. The third course is to rake in the sewers of history in search of anything that can be used to malign, ridicule and belittle and then to compound the discoveries into what can be made to appear a damning indictment. No prolonged human endeavour fails to provide material for the scavengers.

* * * *

There is no need to delve deeply into Athenian life, and even less into the life of its successor whose torch it lit, before coming upon dark, unlovely, hideous things. Yet men speak of the glory that was Greece and the splendour that was Rome. That is surely the true significance of these great civilisational watersheds—the first, a tremendous flowering of the spirit of man; the second, an inspirational genius for the fashioning of legal and administrative systems which, however modified, have been and are still guiding-lights for the governance of human society. If this much be granted, do we need to wait for upwards of two thousand years before men of comprehensive insight look back to discover the glory and the splendour and the rich compassion that was Imperial Britain? Surely not.

To follow the second course and strike a balance would be difficult. The criterion of judgement alone, the arrival at agreed premises, are matters more for the schoolman than for evaluation through popular media, which to maintain interest require clearer outlines. The third course, however, presents no problems. Dirt lies everywhere for those who seek it, and the nearer the seekers are to the ground the less they need to exert themselves to find it. Those of us whose business it is to study political "form" had no doubt whatever as to which course the B.B.C. would take.

I was abroad when the series began and am only now able to catch up because not all the thunder of criticism has deterred Charles Curran from allowing it to be repeated—it would seem that for some unrevealed purpose the denigration of our imperial past is more important that the anger of the British people.

The first production purported to tell the story of our rule in the Caribbean. That rule consisted, it seems, not only of slavery but of the

11

systematic torturing of slaves. They were flogged. They were placed in tormenting iron collars. Every slave-owner was a monster. The relationship was not, as I had been naive enough to believe, in general paternalistic. When Big Brother demands horror, then horror is the order of the day. Nelson, we are told, approved of slavery. There was even a slight suggestion, or so I thought, that in some queer way Trafalgar had been fought for the benefit of the wicked planters!

* * * *

Dr. Cameron Hazlehurst, Research Assistant of the series, had stated that it was "conceived as an evocation of the late Victorian imperial experience", but its editor —Max Morgan-Witts—travelled a long way from that concept. One or two apologists have also sought to involve the Victorians, perhaps being unaware that the British Parliament had abolished slavery before Victoria ascended the throne and thirty years before the Civil War brought it to an end in the United States. As the British West Indies continued under Crown Colony rule for a century and a half after all slaves had been freed, the motive of the B.B.C. in broadcasting a production relating their history almost entirely in terms of slavery —and the most bestial slavery, too—must be held suspect.

The production dealing with Darkest Africa also introduced the slavery theme, a commentator sententiously reminding viewers of Britain's share in this abominable trade. If the makers of the series are as concerned about slaves as they would like to suggest, why do they not throw up their lucrative jobs in London and go campaigning in those parts of Arabia where slaves are still bought and sold and most cruelly treated?

There was nothing in the Darkest Africa feature concerning the imperial *motif* which related to the Victorians and what was Victorian had nothing to do with the British Empire!

Livingstone, Burton and Speke were explorers, not empire builders. The sole imperial enterprise depicted was the arrival in the Eastern Cape of the 1820 settlers, seventeen years before the accession of Queen Victoria. The defeat at Weenan of Dingaan's impis, to which the production gives well-earned honour, was an epic of Afrikaner courage and the British had nothing to do with it. As the B.B.C. team contrived, against every known fact, to extend the sway of Lord Charles Somerset to embrace Zululand, it may have supposed that the Boers fought under British auspices!

In the programme on the carving up of Africa the bright boys hit upon the idea of making it appear as a game of dice, taking great care heavily to load the dice —against Britain. The British defeat at Majuba in the first Boer War was stressed out of all proportion to the general theme, as was the annihilation of a small British column taken by surprise by the Zulus at Isandhlwana. Lord Chelmsford's final victory at Ulundi was dismissed in a sentence, and there was no mention of the heroic defence at Rorkes Drift, which led to the bestowal of seven V.C.s.

The second Boer War allowed the B.B.C. denigrators really to "go to town". Initial British reverses were gloatingly related, much emphasis was placed on the burning of farm-houses and the "concentration camps" and even after the capture of Pretoria we were assured that the British were defeated "again and again and again". As Kimberley was presented mainly as a sort of brothel, with can-can dances, illimitable gambling and abundant prostitution, so were the British troops in South Africa ridiculed by frequent resort to music-halls and the patriotic songs now long outdated. One such effort—obviously a comic song in the great Cockney tradition—which concerned a

Tommy asking to go back overseas, "where the Boers can't get at me", was sung as a serious matter which revealed the low morale of the British troops in South Africa! It was a disgusting slander.

All this slanted stuff could not have been interpreted as anything other than blatantly and venomously anti-British, but what more than anything revealed the B.B.C.s utter dishonesty was that in mentioning the names of the most famous Boer generals those of the two greatest were omitted—Smuts and Botha. Could it have been because in later life they became staunch upholders of the British Empire? No other explanation is possible. Beyond any doubt whatever, the B.B.C. had no intent other than to make cheap and tawdry the entire British achievement not only in Africa but everywhere else in the world.

Although not treasonable in the legal sense it stands charged with high treason in every spiritual sense.

The production devoted to India was atrocious. Men and women of any true intellectual calibre, possessing a knowledge of the facts, can only wonder at the magnificent achievement of the British Raj, and before that of the British East India Company. When the programme began with a picture of the Khyber Pass I expected to hear a tribute to Tommy Atkins, who for so long had stood sentinel there to keep the Afghans and frontier tribes from raiding and despoiling the people it was his duty to protect. Instead, with its deadly instinct for humiliation, the B.B.C. at once switched to the eastern frontier to announce, with what sounded a shout of triumph, that Japan's victories in Malaya and Burma had ground Britain's prestige irrecoverably into the Indian dirt. That the Fourteenth Army was to drive the enemy from these countries received no mention, being "out of context" perhaps!

Dr. Hazlehurst throws some astonishing light on the team's attitude towards the British in India. The script at first read : "Triggered off by religious feelings, the Mutiny provided predictable atrocities which inflamed British opinion". After the word "atrocities", we are told, Morgan-Witts cautiously interpolated three words : "on both sides". Dr. Hazlehurst appears to think this was an admirable way of "avoiding obvious partiality". Well, of course, we know the B.B.C. well enough to be aware that its time-dishonoured tradition is to ensure complete "impartiality" by the simple device of damning the British.

As one instance of how the method works, no more than a single reference was made to the slaughter of 140 British women in Cawnpore and not one to their children who were hacked to pieces with them. There was visual representation of the capture of the women, on the river-bank, but their fate thereafter was mentioned almost as an incidental. Contrast this with the loving concentration of the cameras on the ceremony of executing a mutineer at the cannon's mouth. The full rites were carried through in stately measure to the accompanying of drum-beats and close-ups showed every twitch on the condemned man's face. Viewers must have gained the impression that what mattered was not the slaughter of British women (the children not being mentioned) but the brutality of the British in bringing such pomp and panoply of power to bear upon the punishment of a sepoy—who looked, by the way, as though he had been specially chosen for his mildness of countenance. Such is the B.B.C.s lack of bias!

Bias was apparent again in the depiction of the relief of Lucknow. The arrival of the Campbells had in it about as much verve and drama as a convocation of the Flat Earth Society. They advanced in a strange kind of open order, which would have ensured that in action those in front were shot by one or other of the several lines behind them—a matter not put to the test because they seemingly had no opposition to overcome! Then followed a ludicrous patter-patter of feet as kilted legs were shown endlessly trotting up the steps of the battlement. This pitiful charade was in marked contrast to the vivid charges of the Zulu hosts at Weenan. It may be that the very superior young men who made up the B.B.C. team disdained the idea that British troops in battle show dynamism and dash.

The tendency throughout the programme was falsely to emphasise clashes between ruler and ruled and quite a lot of lathis were shown at work. There was little indication that throughout the period of Raj young British District Commissioners and their seniors stood between the Indian peasants and the grasping Indian landlords and moneylenders, while tiny British garrisons kept the overall peace. The one tribute to them was swamped by ludicrous trivia about the equipment they took when travelling in "comfort."

* * * *

There was grudging mention of some good work done by the British Rai, but nothing to convey the magnitude of the task and the magnificence in coping with it of the most highly skilled and devoted civil servants ever sent by one country to serve the needs of another. "Not a bad record," the commentator was nevertheless condescending enough to admit.

What I found particularly galling was the programme's investment of the man who brought the Raj to an end with the great qualities of the man who had been its creator. Clive marched 500 men to Arcot whence he drove a French-led Army ten thousand strong, and withstood a subsequent siege with unsurpassed leadership and valour. His generalship at Plassey won for Britain—and indeed for India— two hundred years of the most beneficial use of imperial power the world has ever known. What comparable triumphs had the last Pro-Consul to show? Dieppe? Or the two million dead after Hindus and Moslems had fallen upon each other to celebrate the result of his insouciant statesmanship in handling over a sub-continent to anarchy and riot?

* * * *

The contemptuous playing down of the wonderful British achievement in India gave way, in the programme about Canada, to sheer mindlessness. Nothing whatever indicated the creation of a young and virile nation with a great destiny ahead of it. Wolfe was written off as a weak, indecisive, neurotic man and his great victory on the Heights of Abraham was shown as much of a charade as the relief of Lucknow. The French were depicted advancing almost in a slow march, but the B.B.C. did concede that Wolfe had trained his men to withhold fire until the enemy were twenty-five yards, a tactic which called "as much for nerve as for skill'—so much for the neurotic character of the man who won Canada from the French ! Otherwise—nothingness. The opening up of these vast territories was allowed to go almost entirely by default. However, the American War of 1812 did enable the B.B.C. to have another crack at Britain during its programme on Canada. We were told that the Americans at sea "over and over again" defeated the British Navy which covered itself with glory at Trafalgar. What we were not told is that between 1805 and 1812 the French had built a new fleet, sixty sail-of-the-line, and that the vital task of British sea-power was to watch and contain it, so that we had very little in reserve to support our land forces in America. The defeats encountered were in small engagements, the largest being fought at squadron strength. It may be that in addition to serving its own anti-British bias, the B.B.C. wanted to feed American pride for the gratification of Time/Life Incorporated, in association with whom the entire series was produced.

17

I have not seen the production which dealt with Australia, but my friends who have—and all Australians whose views I have read—were livid with frustration and rage at what they took to be an almost obscene parody of this splendid young nation. The idea conveyed was of a population consisting in the main of highly eccentric drop-outs. Can the B.B.C. really derive pleasure from the knowledge that it has managed to drive yet another wedge between the Mother Country and the land which bred the heroes of Gallipoli and the Somme? As for the programme on New Zealand, there could be no weightier criticism than that of Sir Bernard Fergusson, a former Governor-General, who "found its standards of taste deplorable" and who challenged its facts.

* * * *

Ending his letter on a general note, Sir Bernard wrote: "I cannot conceive what the purpose behind this series can be, unless it is to make us ashamed, and our children, of what is not an inglorious past. It is the perquisite of the propagandist, not of the historian, to select and perpetuate only the shadiest pages of the record." Mr. Louis Heren made much the same point in an article published by *The Times*. He said that he could not forgive the producer his "lack of a sense of history and humanity". Lord Ferrier wrote in support: "It is quite misleading to imply that the attack on the series is nothing but the fashion. The fact is that the inadequacies of the programmes (admitted to some extent by the Director-General) have caused widespread indignation, well illustrated by the B.B.C.s own *Talk Back* programme on March 29. Speaking for myself the depth of my unease is partly due to a sense of loss of the respect in which I have hitherto held the B.B.C. It would appear that Messrs. Curran, Attenborough and Singer [B.B.C. apologists—Ed.] are blind to the damage which has been done to the standing of the Corporation. . . ."

Even more damning was the verdict of Sir George Schuster: "To state all the grounds for criticising the series would require a very long letter. I content myself with two observations. (1) whatever- criticisms may be justified of some of the policies of Whitehall or of some examples of the social behaviour of British commercial circles in overseas territories, the world's history of colonial administrations has never contained so notable an example of devoted service in the interests of, and in friendly relations with, the local populations, as that given by the British members of the Civil Service in India, the Crown Colonies, and the Sudan. (2) The series has provided in a very special way an illustration of the terrifying monopoly power for using television to influence public opinion which rests with B.B.C. producers. I emphasize the epithet 'terrifying'. Terrifying is the exact word. "

The talk-back referred to by Lord Ferrier was an assembly gathered for a confrontation with those responsible for the Empire series. Except for the Features Editor, who was inclined to become petulant, the team seemed to be somewhat suave young men who genuinely had no idea of the enormity of their disservice to the British people. I feel sure that even after the lambastings they received on that occasion, and the general nation-wide protest, they still feel that they had done a good job of work. Their inability to understand the true greatness of the British achievement was total. They did have the grace, however, to listen with courtesy to their critics, who minced no words in saying what they thought about the project. Unfortunately their good manners were not matched by Michael Barrett, who presided. This B.B.C. functionary was responsible for a disgraceful incident.

One of the critics was an elderly man, distinguished in bearing and of obvious intellectual calibre, who subjected the series to an enlightened analysis and gave a considered opinion of the gross impropriety, not only of producing it, but of doing so in association with Time/Life Inc, with its built-in American bias against the Imperial Power which had laid the foundation of the American nation. The team being unable to meet reason by reason, Barrett came to its rescue. Putting on his most unctuous smile, he leant towards the elderly man and said in a soothing voice: "I am sure you will not mind my mentioning it, sir, but you *are* 81, are you not?"

* * * *

That was just about the most bounderish remark that even the B.B.C. has managed to put over the air. It could mean only one of two things—either that the man thus addressed was gagga (a preposterous idea) or that age and long experience invalidated his views (which in rather a different way is no less preposterous). Is truth dependent on the age of its exponent? Do matters such as taste, ethical judgement and sense of history pass beyond the purview of people by virtue of the fact that they have grown older and wiser than Mr. Barrett (who himself would appear not to be in his pristine vigour)? At what age does Pundit Barrett expect to be written off as one whose views no longer count?

When the clamour of indignation was first heard, Director-General Curran no doubt hoped, as over Northern Ireland, to ride the storm, but once again this proved too difficult. He felt obliged to make a public statement, and a very curious statement it was. The series, one gathered, did not meet with his unreserved approval. One or two of the programmes had rather disappointed him, it seems—the one on Canada in particular, because he "knew something about Canada". Great Heavens, is it possible that there should be a Director General of the British Broadcasting Corporation who does not know a great deal about every British land? The most significant passage in the

Curran statement was: "The *British Empire* series hasn't actually offended everybody—but let us suppose that it had. All that one needs to conclude from that is that it wasn't perhaps the best series we have ever produced. In other words, it is a question about the execution of a programme intention, not a question about the nature of the B.B.C." It is here that Charles Curran goes completely off the rails. Close students of B.B.C. form could have predicted with certainty that any such programme would be handled with a lofty disdain of the great traditional values, that where it was inexpedient to be blatantly hostile care would be exercised to belittle and subtly traduce the high endeavours of our sires, and that no discoverable dirt would be left unraked.

* * * *

Indeed, B.B.C. form was so firmly established during the thirties that when the war came, imposing upon it the need to evoke the spirit of patriotism, the lofty internationalists then running the show were completely at a loss. Their floundering was pathetic. So, at base, has it always been whenever a call came to assert the British cause in the face of internationalist displeasure. There is no need to search the past for proof. Claiming that the Empire series' listening public of eight millions represented a "considerable achievement", Charles Curran did not allow the anger of the British people to prevent him from having the disgraceful, soiling enterprise repeated all over again by B.B.C.1. That he should have gone ahead without regard to the sense of national outrage would indicate, not only that his own quantitative valuation serves as his yard-stick, but that the B.B.C. is assured of support from those in the highest positions of power in the land, and perhaps not in this land alone. Time/Life wields no small influence.

Besides, though the Empire series may be the most towering evidence to date of the B.B.C.s motivation, it is by no means the only contemporary example. Last year there was the repulsive denigration of Cecil Rhodes by a creature who had crawled through the sewers of history in an endeavour to find credence for the three-fold lie that Rhodes was a homosexual, a gun-running traitor and a coward. All the Britons who brought civilisation to the country now called Rhodesia were besmirched in the same programme. In the serial still running called *The Regiment* yet another foul attack was made on Cecil Rhodes, and also—as it would appear to me—on pretty well the entire British Army engaged in the South African War. Having spent seven years of my life on active service I can claim to have supped as full of horrors as most men and encountered as many bizarre situations, but never in all that time have I come across the kind of insanity which this serial attributes to British officers, or the gruesome characteristics with which it invests British N.C.O.s and rankers. Why does the B.B.C. *have* to do this sort of thing? Why, why, why?

* * * *

The time has come for an answer to be found to this question. At the very least responsibility for the Empire series insult was not seen to be shrugged off when *The Times* published this unobtrusive paragraph. "Mr. Max Morgan-Witts, editor of the B.B.C.s controversial television series on the British Empire, is leaving the corporation at his own request to write a book, the corporation announced last night." The only comment that one would wish to make on this minor casualty is an expression of regret that the same literary urge did not precipitate others much higher up the scale to enrich the library of anti-British defamation within the restricted confines of a book.

At any rate *The Times* has done a public service by bringing the entire issue into the open. It asks in a leading article: "Who should run the B.B.C.?" This brings us, if not to the crux, at any rate close to it. The newspaper quotes the definition of the role of the Corporation's governors given by Lord Normanbrook, a former chairman. The governors, he said, are the ultimate authority and the "trustees for the national interest" with responsibility for the overall quality of the broadcasting services. The board, he pointed out, determines policy and "takes the final decisions on all major questions of management and on all matters of controversy which may arouse strong feeling in Parliament or among large sections of public opinion".

Assuming Lord Normanbrook to be right, it will be seen that if a national disgrace such as the wholesale insulting of the British Empire had power to create a revolution, standing-room in the tumbrils would assuredly be required for Lord Hill and his fellow governors. It is in that event they who have besmirched the name of Cecil John Rhodes. It is they, even now, who are making *Grand Guignol* characters of British Tommies in the Boer War. More than that, it is they who have taken sexual intercourse from the privacy wherein even primitive peoples confine it and staged it on a lawn for millions of people to see how beautiful experience can be made ugly and debased. The question, therefore, is not so much who should run the B.B.C. as who can be trusted to select governors fitted for the responsibility of so high a duty. That problem out of the way, attention should be devoted to the kind of man required to serve as Director-General. Let Mr. Curran he judged by his programmes. I know nothing of him apart from what he authorises and therefore say no more.

* * * *

23

Here, however, is a strange insight into the character of his predecessor. It concerns Mrs. Whitehouse, a campaigner for propriety in public life who has been battling against recent invitations by the B.B.C. to Tariq Ali and Devlin to impart their anti-British views to the listening world. Down through the years Mrs. Whitehouse has come into collision with Broadcasting House in her efforts to stop its standards from galloping deterioration. I quote from the *Sunday People* "Mrs. Mary Whitehouse, 60-year-old television clean-up crusader, is about to be painted as a full-frontal nude. At the urgent request of her old enemy, former B.B.C. director-general Sir Hugh Greene. Sir Hugh, who is 61, has commissioned the painting from artist Lawrence Isherwood, of Wigan. "She always hated me," Sir Hugh wrote to Mr. Isherwood, "and I always refused to have anything to do with her. It would be pleasant, now, to have her naked on my walls." Artist Isherwood has hired a model to pose for the naked body. She a 33-year-old woman. The face of Mrs. Whitehouse will be painted from photographs. Sir Hugh, who lives near Bury St. Edmunds, Suffolk, chose from a batch of preliminary sketches submitted by the artist. In the one he chose, Mrs. Whitehouse has five breasts. Mrs. Whitehouse, at home at Far Forest, Worcestershire, said yesterday "This is beneath reasonable consideration." That was a dignified reply, but should the matter in fact not be taken into very grave consideration? It concerns one to whom the Governors delegated what Sir George has rightly called the "terrifying" monopoly power of the B.B.C. Sir Hugh Greene's father was my headmaster. I did not think him an inspiring pedagogue, but he never struck me as being other than a gentleman, which word I use in the context, not of class, but of character. Genes, it would seem, do not always run true to form.

Here, I think, is the real crux. Would not the problem of the B.B.C. be greatly diminished if it could be placed in the charge of a Director-General who—besides being a natural patriot, sufficiently informed and perceptive to understand the sinister power of evil to bend and corrupt—was also a gentleman?

It would perhaps not be realistic to advocate that the Corporation should be swept into limbo and replaced by some different body, but its radical reform is essential. Could it not be reconstructed and re-staffed in such a way that the spirit of its highest achievements—the spirit, let us say, which animated *The Forsyte Saga* - pervaded all other departments, especially those concerned with politico-historical documentaries and topical comment?

* * * *

We cannot go on as we are. The B.B.C. defames our past, poisons our present and places our future at desperate hazard. No nation can survive which is conditioned by a vast fifth-column serving forces which have a vested interest in its obliteration as a sovereign, independent Realm. There is not much time left. The best immediate news would the resignation of Lord Hill, his colleagues and those of his subordinates who have proved unworthy of the trust placed in them by a still great and mighty people.

In a still more urgent sense than the occasion on which Leopold Amery used the words, we say to them—For God's sake, Go!

About A.K. Chesterton

Arthur Kenneth Chesterton was born at the Luipaards Vlei gold mine, Krugersdorp, South Africa where his father was an official in 1899.

In 1915 unhappy at school in England A.K. returned to South Africa. There and without the knowledge of his parents, and having exaggerated his age by four years, he enlisted in the 5th South African Light Infantry.

Before his 17th birthday he had been in the thick of three battles in German East Africa. Later in the war he transferred as a commissioned officer to the Royal Fusiliers and served for the rest of the war on the Western Front being awarded the Military Cross in 1918 for conspicuous gallantry.

Between the wars A.K. first prospected for diamonds before becoming a journalist first in South Africa and then England. Alarmed at the economic chaos threatening Britain, he joined Sir Oswald Mosley in the B.U.F and became prominent in the movement. In 1938, he quarrelled with Mosley's policies and left the movement.

When the Second World War started he rejoined the army, volunteered for tropical service and went through all the hardships of the great push up from Kenya across the wilds of Jubaland through the desert of the Ogaden and into the remotest parts of Somalia. He was afterwards sent down the coast to join the Somaliland Camel Corps and intervene in the inter-tribal warfare among the Somalis.

In 1943 his health broke down and he was invalided out of the army with malaria and colitis, returning to journalism. In 1944, he became deputy editor and chief leader writer of *Truth*.

In the early 1950s A.K. established *Candour* and founded the League of Empire Loyalists which for some years made many colourful headlines in the press worldwide. He later took that organisation into The National Front, and served as its Chairman for a time.

A.K. Chesterton died in 1973.

About *The A.K. Chesterton Trust*

The A.K. Chesterton Trust was formed by Colin Todd and the late Miss. Rosine de Bounevialle in January 1996 to succeed and continue the work of the now defunct Candour Publishing Co.

The objects of the Trust are stated as follows:

"To promote and expound the principles of A.K. Chesterton which are defined as being to demonstrate the power of, and to combat the power of International Finance, and to promote the National Sovereignty of the British World."

Our aims include:

- *Maintaining and expanding the range of material relevant to A.K. Chesterton and his associates throughout his life.*

- *To preserve and keep in-print important works on British Nationalism in order to educate the current generation of our people.*

- *The maintenance and recovery of the sovereign independence of the British Peoples throughout the world.*

- *The strengthening of the spiritual and material bonds between the British Peoples throughout the world.*

- *The resurgence at home and abroad of the British spirit.*

We will raise funds by way of merchandising and donations.

We ask that our friends make provision for *The A.K. Chesterton Trust* in their will.

The A.K. Chesterton Trust has a **duty** to keep *Candour* in the ring and punching.

CANDOUR: To defend national sovereignty against the menace of international finance.

CANDOUR: To serve as a link between Britons all over the world in protest against the surrender of their world heritage.

Subscribe to Candour

CANDOUR SUBSCRIPTION RATES FOR 10 ISSUES.

U.K. £25.00
Europe 40 Euros.
Rest of the World £35.00.
USA $50.00.

All Airmail. Cheque's and Postal Orders, £'s Sterling only, made payable to *The A.K. Chesterton Trust.* (Others, please send cash by **secure post**, $ bills or Euro notes.)

Payment by Paypal is available. Please see our website **www.candour.org.uk** for more information.

Candour Back Issues

Back issues are available. 1953 to the present.

Please request our back issue catalogue by sending your name and address with two 1st class stamps to:

The A.K. Chesterton Trust, BM Candour, London, WC1N 3XX, UK

Alternatively, see our website at **www.candour.org.uk** where you can order a growing selection on-line.

The A.K. Chesterton Trust Reprint Series

1. Creed of a Fascist Revolutionary & Why I Left Mosley - A.K. Chesterton.

2. The Menace of World Government & Britain's Graveyard - A.K. Chesterton.

3. What You Should Know About The United Nations - The League of Empire Loyalists.

4. The Menace of the Money-Power - A.K. Chesterton.

5. The Case for Economic Nationalism - John Tyndall.

6. Sound the Alarm! - A.K. Chesterton.

7. Six Principles of British Nationalism - John Tyndall.

8. B.B.C. - A National Menace - A.K. Chesterton

9. Stand By The Empire - A.K. Chesterton

Other Titles from *The A.K. Chesterton Trust*

Leopard Valley - A.K. Chesterton

Juma The Great - A.K. Chesterton

The New Unhappy Lords - A.K. Chesterton

Facing The Abyss - A.K. Chesterton

The History of the League of Empire Loyalists - McNeile & Black

All the above titles are available from The A.K. Chesterton Trust, BM Candour, London, WC1N 3XX, UK

www.candour.org.uk

Printed in Great Britain
by Amazon